Everyone's a Star after Midnight

Wayne Power

First Published in 2020 by The Manuscript Publisher

ISBN: 978-1-911442-25-7

A CIP Catalogue record for this book is available from the National Library

Typesetting, page design and layout, cover design by DocumentsandManuscripts.com

Cover photography by Hayley K Stuart

Published, printed and bound in Ireland

Everyone's a Star after Midnight

Copyright © Wayne Power, 2020

Dedications

For Mam and Dad

Clive, Ian, Craig, Michael, Liam and Bryan

My sister, Aoife

My nieces, Caoimhe, Millie and Eabha

My grandparents

Light up another cig
'Cos, we dream big.
Sleep to dream; wake to chase them
Like the dusk chases the moon
For, everyone's a star after midnight.
Spark up another cig
'Cos, we dream big, to live bigger and love better.
Everyone's a star after midnight,
Chasing dreams like moths chase the light.
Everyone's a star after midnight.
Pin your dream to the heart on your sleeve and
Let the dreamcatcher weave its magic and its
Twists of fate. Dream big; it's never too late.
Sleep to dream; wake to chase.
We dream big, with tears down our face.
We dream big. We dream bright.

Everyone's a star after midnight.

Contents

State of the Nation

Vote Number 1. I'll knock on your door and
whore myself out for your vote, forgetting all the
women who had to take the boat.
Confession box has no seal. Papa don't preach.
See no evil, hear no evil about how the priest
had a cheeky feel but, they'll scream from the
pulpit about repeal.
And still the Holy Joes, caked in woes, will stand
outside a clinic to taunt a pregnant woman seeking
a termination: that's just the state of this nation.
Bless me father for he/him have sinned. Told the
world he was trans and he got chinned, binned –
a public offender all because they didn't
choose their gender.
Dead bodies on a trolley. If you take a right past
The Folly, bad moods and leaky fluids, pile up a
Corridor. No sanctuary, no mortuary.
Where's the light when you've got nowhere to
sleep tonight? There but by the grace of God, into
a cramped hotel room and tell the kids, Santa will
still visit. Write him a letter and ask him to make
it better.
Toxic banks and septic tanks, dodgy loans and
lying planks and yet, we still give thanks.
Knock, knock. Who's there?
"Your local candidate, here to sell his ware."
"Tell me what you can deliver. Will you stop my
unemployed son from jumping in the river

because, he had a dream and yet now, he's stuck
on a CE scheme? Went to the hospital 'cos he
wanted to end it all. Was told, there's no bed here,
go home, here's a tablet, sleep it off. Goes out
and gets pissed 'cos he's six months on a
waiting list. Depressed, waiting to be assessed.
Landlord's been around and his telly has been
Repossessed."

Deadbeats, dodgy streets, as the politician smiles
and greets, "Jobs for you, house for you, I
promise, I swear. Vote Number 1, I care. Vote
Number 1, I dare."

Alienation, isolation, desolation, one more
protest, no consolation.

Vote Number 1, for the state of the nation.

Tear Up the Dancefloor

Ariana Grande, Emeli Sande –
That shit's all a bit bland, eh!
Fighting off little pricks, bopping to Little Mix,
I'll be the whore to tear up the dancefloor.
And what's more, when I wake in the morning
And my head's sore and I ask myself, "Did I
score?"
Sure, I was the one who let a roar –
Tear up the dancefloor.
Getting the shift to Taylor Swift. Shake it off and
shake what yer oul wan gave ya, in full pissed-
up mode to Old Town Road. Some wan on her
hen night, in full flight, getting felt up by some
gobshite. Tear up the dancefloor with all your
might: a smooch, a dance, Lady Gaga's 'Bad Romance'
catching a glance. Another drink. Fool yourself you're
in with a chance but, you won't get a dare
'cos, "surprise, surprise", he's straight
and it's getting late, and the alcohol is
gonna sedate the demons and the doubt. Tear up
the dancefloor 'cos, "I'm out, out."
Britney Spears, drunken tears, pervy leers, few
more beers, dance away your fears, conversing
drunkenly with peers, late night heartache
swaying to Drake, Uptown Funk. "Who's the hunk?"
Would love a bunk. Bet he's got something I can
dunk 'cos, I'm done living like a monk. Billie
Jean, scene queen, looking lean. There's some

fella acting the creep, sniffing round some wan
who he wants to plough balls deep and yet, with all the
    drink,
she can barely stand and your man is mad to
drop the hand. Bopping his head to another
covers band, the best nights are not planned. Yer
man was mad to drop the hand, drop the jaw,
bang her raw only, she hit him a clatter, dropped
the glass to shatter. She calls him a prick. The
boys are giving him wicked stick, taking the Mick.
Your wan is fit to give him a kick in the sack.
"Sure, I'm only having the craic," he pleads as his
nose bleeds and he concedes that it just wasn't
his night. When you're acting the gobshite
And yer wan is still bitching in the taxi, "That fella
is stink. I grew up with him down the Group Link.
Did ya see him giving me the wink and he
reeking of drink; he'd want to see a shrink.
Making a pass at me at this hour, I tell ya, he can
go hang his balls off the Clock Tower."
The morning after, I reminisce in the uproar and,
"Yeah, the heads sore. Ring me later and we'll go
tear up the dancefloor."

Snackbox

Fresh fade, self-made, night raid.
Beaming, creaming, scheming, redeeming,
Dreaming.
Chewing the ear, chewing the jaw, in awe of the
saints and sinners. One more round; we're all
winners.
"Didn't see you for years," knocking back beers.
Some girl in tears eyeing up other queers and a
pair of eyes that sears.
Hash clouds and shit talk. Can't find a taxi; might
Walk.
Gards on the beat. Wobbly on my feet. Packed
Street.
Getting pally down Spring Garden Alley. Drunken
tangle down the Viking Triangle. Dancing and
swerving, "Is yer man still serving?" Bouncers
pulling someone aside for a few quiet words.
Boys and girls, dirt birds.
"Have you met such and such?" "Ah yeah, sure."
"Keep in touch."
Swapping numbers, swapping skins, swapping
tongues,
Off his rig, hitting a dig, going to some gig. Got a
light for this cig. Horsing into a chip like a pig.
Wander Inn, stagger out, drunken smackers on
the mouth. "Sure, I'll see you out. Give us a shout.
Keep them sweet 'cos I've heard they've got
clout." Pissing away the doubt. Another pint

bottle. Complete the rout.
Coming from the school of hard knocks.
Hit the jax, grab a taxi, small talk to a stranger,
Snackbox.

Man About Town

Another man on the town, acting the clown.
Out with all the blokes. Gets his fade from Val Stokes.
A night on the rip. Still waiting on Liverpool to win
the Premiership.
In bits over a pair of tits. A chip on the way home and
    wake up with the shits
and his boss is throwing fits 'cos, he comes into work like a
    box of Lego – in bits.
'Cos he's a man about the town. In his nine to five
he's gonna drown. Sure, he's just another waster,
another clown, on the beer, a bit of gear, keeps
it all bottled up, all that fear, the hidden tear.
And he'll veer from The Mansion to Philly Grimes,
pissing against walls and shouting rhymes, till he
finds the girl he marries, the odd ride, a night in
Kathy Barry's.
He ain't got no plan, the King of Waterford. Loves
his county like John Mullane. Sees a girl and lets
his eyes linger, till he's at the back of Lombard
Street chipper, slipping her the finger at 2 in the
morning, kissing and fawning 'cos the girls got a
pussy like a hippo yawning but, he can't say a
word 'cos he's been around the block so, don't slut
shame the girl 'cos she likes a bit of cock.
And the next day, he's on the cure, wondering if
what's up his nose is pure. Half of it, he's already
sniffed, just to get him through another 12-hour
shift, working on the line as Beat blast out

another one from Taylor Swift. Goes out for a
fag, gives the boys a slag 'cos Liverpool are 12
points clear. "Yeah boy, fuck United. Sure, Ole
Gunnar is a ginger queer."

And at the weekend, the boys are on the bang (all
the gang) and he's eyeing up the blonde in the
skirt, buys her a drink, a cheeky flirt, lovely
yungwan, she's been through the mill, she's been
hurt, her last fella did the dirt and he's telling her
she should know her worth. So, she knocks back
another gin and gets a taxi home alone.

And he's sitting there on The Plaza, staggering
around like Gazza.

Sobering up, he can feel himself drown. Feel
the voices drag him down and, would he finally
be free if he climbed over the barrier and flung
himself in The Quay?

And sometimes the sun comes up and he can
feel the depression hit but, lift your head up, boy.
I'm telling you now, keep her lit.

Urinal Conversing

I can't even take a piss anymore
Without some fucker swaying into me,
"I know your father, your brother and your
mother. And yer oul wan's mother.
Dead now, God love her."
And he's getting my name wrong but, I'm more
focused on dousing the blue cubes in the urinal
in yellow liquid and having another pint.
And he stinks of drink and is cribbing about his missus.
"Women, boy, they break your heart."
"Tell me about it," I reply, as if I'm some sort of
Casanova, when the last woman who broke my
heart was Geri Halliwell when she left the Spice Girls
and little does he know, I haven't seen a vagina since birth.
And as I look down, my eyes meet his whiskey dick
and I'm thinking, it's no wonder his missus is cribbing.
"Do ya still play the hurling?"
"Ah no," I say because I never could wield a stick
but these days, I still like to take a pull on a fella.
And he's bitching about Austin Gleeson,
for no reason, calling him overrated and I'm thinking,
could you do any better with your five bellies and bingo
    wings.
"Bring Derek back," he roars.
"Derek who?" I think out loud, thinking, is he
referring to local author, Derek Flynn or comedy
icon, Derek Trotter?
And at this stage, the cubicle adjacent is a

revolving door of snorted nostrils and staggering
fools, revelling in shit talk and drunken bravado.
"The town is full of them," he continues.
"Full of what?" I say and at this point, he
launches into a diatribe about foreigners and "all
that crowd coming in, getting everything" but, he
will still have no problem handing over a tenner
to some African driver in three hours' time, to take
him and the missus home,
Just before he stops for a takeaway from a
sweet Polish girl.
"But they have great bodies though," he smirks
as if he'd stand a chance and I can't agree with
him because, I don't do much looking before he
starts singing at the dirty tiles on the wall
"Don't Stop Believing" by Journey or, the cast of
Glee, if you're a pop culture obsessed
homosexual averse to a musical number or three.
"Never stop believing, boy. Sinn Féin never
stopped believing, boy. They're gonna sort this country
    out boy."
At this stage, I'm eyeing up the guy at the hand dryer with
the mohawk and stubble and wondering,
Does he take the same bus as me
and if he does, is he top deck or bottom deck?
And to my surprise, he throws me a nod that
neither confirms nor denies and I see an
opportunity, a tiny glimmer of hope at quarter
past 12 on a Saturday night.
"Town is full of them too," says your man.
"Full of what?" I says.
"Queers!" he snarls.
And as I pull the zip up on my skinny jeans, I look

directly at him and grin,
"I know, boy. Int it fucking great?"
And I walk out, full of Heineken and full of hope
and full of whatever this night might bring.
And I can still hear him singing, Don't Stop
Believing, which is apt
'Cos, I never fucking stopped.
"Pint of Heineken, girl. Sound."

These Streets

These streets
Are the blood that courses through my veins
And makes my heart beat.
These streets
Are the rain-battered windows
On lonely nights, laying on lonely sheets.
These streets
Are the remedy and the balm
When the anxiety cheats and bleats
On a loop and tries to dupe you
Into thinking you're not strong enough.
These streets
Are the legacy we build and leave behind:
The 9 to 5, the daily grind, the tracks of our years
The laughs, the tears, the dark black clouds that
carried our fears. These streets are the songs that
echo in our ears over spilled beers and, whatever
way your crazy, rebel heart veers.
These streets
Are the chased pavements, the cracked
Footpaths, we tread our weary feet on, as life
goes on. These streets are the best laid plans
with a couple of cans.
These streets are what made me, saved me and
shaped me. These streets are the unanswered
prayers, the layers we hide behind, the truth we
find.
These streets are the lives we lead, the noose

we freed, the blood we bleed, the air we breathe
the mouths we feed, the eyes we read, the
defeats we concede, the terms we agreed, the
love we need, the dog off the lead, our colours,
our creed.
These streets
Are our blood, sweat and tears.
These streets
Are the tracks of our years.

Top of the Town

Up at the top of the town,
There's some clown
Staggering around in the horrors
After stumbling out of Alfie's
For, he's no spring chicken
Wandering around Ballybricken.
There's a rumour going round
Up the top of the town
And it's catching like TB
So, you better drink up and flee
And hop into that taxi.
The boys are doing dockets,
Wiling away the hours
Looking at tellies in Paddy Powers,
Taking shelter from the downpours and showers.
Up at the top of the town
They still reminisce
About the "thrill on the hill"
And the congregation that would spill
From the church on Sunday morning:
God fearing men and women
In their Sunday best for the day of rest.
In front of bacon and cabbage, that dinner plate,
they'll ravage.
And the markets that were wheeling and dealing.
Mrs Cuddihy chatting over the road to Nora Heylin.
Don't ever look down
On the top of the town

And the characters and the lives
That would dispense a frown.
The glory days, heading up to the Ard Rí
In your best frock or gown.
Raise a glass
To the top of the town.

Friend Request

Some bogey who bullied you as a teenager has
added you as a friend.
Creeping on someone you fancy and accidentally
liking a seven-year-old picture of him, from that time
he lived in Australia.
Your auntie sharing pictures of guardian angels,
for good luck.
Your other auntie commenting on drunken
pictures of you and saying how much you look
like your father.
Maria is sharing competitions she'll never win
'cos, she's mad for a new hoover from Soundstore.
Martin and Linda are now in a relationship:
"Congratulations, hun"; "Fab, hun"; Gorgeous, hun".
Martin and Linda break up two weeks later.
Linda doesn't want to talk about it
But, she's updated her status, telling all and
Sundry but, she doesn't want to talk about it.
Johnno puts up twenty videos a day from LadBible
and comments under The Journal about
immigrants whilst sharing pictures of Mo Salah.
Margaret wants to know if anyone wants to buy
her tatty old sofa.
"Ah, you'll easily get rid of that." "Oh Margaret, your
sofa is lovely."
Suzanne is only gas 'cos, it's Halloween and she's
got her Christmas tree up.
Martina was tagged in a photo down in Factory.

She doesn't remember; she was polluted.
"Martina, you look fab"; "Wow, Martina"; "Stunning,
    Martina".
"Martina, where'd you get your top? It's gorgeous."
"Penneys, hun."
Gina has checked herself into Geoff's 'cos she's
out with the girls.
Gina is a gas bitch who loves to share videos of
people slapping off the ground and then tagging
her mates saying,
"Jacinta Flynn, that was us Saturday night."
Bobby has checked himself into Shutter Island
'cos he was on the beer till 4 and had to get up
and do a 12-hour shift.
Joey has marked himself as safe during a
bombing atrocity in Palestine, even though he
lives on Henesseys Road.
Joanne has uploaded another 20 photos of her
new-born child because, she thinks nobody has
seen the 30 pictures she uploaded the night
before.
"Spit of his father, Joanne."
Joanne doesn't know who the father is.
Jean is raising money for the Samaritans despite
the fact that she wouldn't say boo to you on the
street 'cos, she's an ignorant bitch.
Tony is banging on about climate change, even
though he dumps his rubbish behind the bins
next to Tesco –
"I'm just doing me bit."
"Well done, Tony. I don't go near the butchers anymore."
Pat lost a score 'cos Ronaldo scored in injury time –
"Portuguese bender! I could've won a score."

Pat secretly looks at gay porn.

Shauna is beaming 'cos she got 100 likes on the
picture of her in her new dress at the Mayor's Ball.

"Wow, Shauna"; "Fab, Shauna"; "OMG!!!!! Wow,
Shauna".

Paddy and Fiona just got engaged –
300 likes

Despite the fact that nobody likes either of them.

He's riding her sister and she has a face like a slapped arse.

Eileen is back from two weeks in Santa Ponsa.

"Eileen, you're black, you're black. The colour of
ya. You're black. I wouldn't know ya."

Eileen replies, "I don't know meself, hun. I'm like Shirley
Valentine. xxx winkie face emoji."

Log in, delete, add, comment, trying to look your best.

You have one new friend request.

Noi Supereremo

They're singing from their balconies
As their people die and doctors make the call
as to who lives and who dies, and still we sing
A wake-up call from the man above, to cherish
and protect what we love. For we stand on the
brink and I can feel myself sink and overthink.
For it is the talk of every ghost town and I have
fear coursing through my bloodstream, at every
news update, every scroll through social media,
at every cough for, I am now living through a
relentless panic attack, can feel the skin on my
hands crack from the constant washing and
drying and I'm crying. Crying because I'm scared.
Who let the fear back in? Who let the fear win? For
now is the time we don't get to sanitise our
original sin. A time without skin on skin
But, we rise, we fall, we rise again, I don't know
when but, by the grace of God, we rise again.
Noi Supereremo.
We shall overcome and we shall open our
windows and sing into the cruel night, for every
lost soul, for every one it took, for the ground it shook.
Noi Supereremo.
In the dead of night, in the pouring rain, when the
thunder crashes from above, when they hoist the
coffins on their shoulders, when the sun comes
up again.
We shall overcome.

Yesterday

Yesterday the kids went out to play. Now they
stay indoors and watch outside as the trees sway.
Yesterday we laughed in school and played the
fool and now, we long for the disgruntled stare of
an exasperated teacher and a mountain of homework.
Yesterday grandkids could be embraced,
squeezed and kissed. Yesterday was an
opportunity missed.
Yesterday a rally cry was but a whisper in the
Wind over trivialities and needless worry.
Yesterday we ran at a canter and lived our lives in
a hurry.
Yesterday we picked out wedding dresses and
Debs' gowns, sullied sartorial choices with a
frown, before we hit the town.
Yesterday we longed for tomorrow, saw only
open roads and a life without sorrow – a 9 to 5
where we'd beg steal and borrow.
Yesterday we planted our dreams to the sun and
the moon, whilst a troubadour in a packed bar
strummed out another tune.
But we look back now and cry because, yesterday
came too soon.

Dance Again

I feel like I'm grieving for a future that will never
Unfold.
The fear is contagious; the war is here to wage us
But, we shall dance again, spill pints and kiss
and hug and gather round for selfies.
And we will revel on packed streets, be held in
lovers' sheets, for however long our heart beats.
The dawn rises and, we'll bask in the sun
And dance again when it's still daylight at ten.
All we have is each other: father, son, brother,
sister, mother.
The tears will stain our worried eyes
for in the midst and chaos and death,
We shall dance again –
For the stars have not gone out yet.

My Town

You could litter my town with the broken
promises and pledges of the elite, the lies that
could fill the street,
Planning applications, misinformation yet, still
no transformation for, we are the neglected and
the ignored. My town was thrown overboard
when the doors closed on the crystal that we
adored and yet, I'm bored of the promises and
the lies, and the closed mouths that caught no
flies. My town is overlooked and undercooked.
Empty buildings and false dawns, from those
who tell us they will give us this, that and the
other –
North Quays, University status and cardiac care
but when, but where?
Beggars and junkies roam the street. Preachers
in our town square babble but, I think it's time to
rouse the rabble.
My town is my city where the art on the walls
hides the gritty. My town is my city stuck on
repeat so, let's rouse the rabble and pound the
street. My town, my city, blue and white flags
and a charm that's familiar and pretty, in my
town, in my city, where we've heard it all before,
the pledges that are now hollow folklore. My
town is going to drown in broken promises and
big white lies. My town is my city that silently
sighs, whilst another man in a suit cries and

tells us what he will deliver – promises as deep as
the Quay river when all we want is a sliver of
hope and to have more than we lack, to be not
on our knees and be the city where everyone
flees to the big smoke or overseas.
We are left behind but, not so blind to the
soundbites and clichés 'cos bullshit pays and
another TD will line their pockets and take
another pay rise whilst my town dies and the
situation is critical and gone beyond the political,
for it's time to rouse the rabble and come in
from the cold, change the record 'cos it's getting
old because, sometimes it's the fine line between
life and death. My town, my city, rouse the rabble
and hold your breath for, we are tough, beautiful
and not without pity – the blue and white,
my town,
my city.

The Other Side

Seanie is on the bang 'cos, he saw his brother
hang from his bedroom ceiling. Home two
weeks from Australia and told no one how he
was feeling.
Lisa cuts herself with a razor blade, waiting for
the memories to fade: the night her innocence
was taken, just a kid, on the floor, bleeding and
shaking. She sees his face every time the
skin peels but, that's how she deals – tells no one
how she feels.
Paidi thought he had it all, till he pissed it
against a wall and the wife packed up and left
and, Paidi was bereft and the bank swooped in
and took his world away. His head he'll lay in the
men's hostel, hoping for an apostle, to carry him
home but, he'll roam the streets, nurse his
regrets and cry for the man that had it all.
Mickey was laid off, tossed aside, 30
years, blood, sweat, tears, reared the kids on his
own, never took one loan, even when cancer
took the love of his life – the devoted wife. And
now, he sits on the opposite side of a glass
hatch, being tormented to fill out this form, tick
this box, stamp, sign, sign again. "You'll find out
when. Your wife died when."
Johnjo loves the blow: too young to know better,
too scared to be a go getter. Sits in the dark to
shed a tear and rack himself with fear 'cos he's

queer and he can't say it out loud 'cos, if his
family knew and, he and his brother have already
rowed, threatened to disown, suffer in silence,
take the girl out, marry her maybe. Don't
get yourself a name – the shame.
What's on the other side of your door?
Where do you bury your dead?
What ghosts do you keep with you when you turn
the light off and go to bed? What's on the other
side of your smile, your pint glass, your stubbed
out joint when you want to run and hide? How do
you keep trying, swallowing your pride, to make
it through the night?
And the other side?
And when your head's fucked from the wherefores
And the whys, just remember, don't let it take the
light from your eyes.

Afterglow

Replaying the lost nights,
The comedown with the sunrise,
The morning after the shite before.
Did I get up your nose
With the other stuff you hoovered up there?
Drink it down, knock it back,
My wasted youth was a brute
That skinned me alive.
Drink it down, knock it back.
The smouldering embers of a summer
That became one long dancefloor that you tore
up
And tore down. Cider rush made my face blush
but, that won't hush the music and the words we
let into the night, like lanterns in the sky and there
is no regret for, why change what's been? Run
headlong into the night, the sights, the sounds,
the lost, the found, when it all comes back
around.
From a whisper to a scream, don't be afraid to
dream for, it's all I have in my pocket when
you're lighting up the night like a rocket.
Drink it down, knock it back.
Happy tears for all the craic.
Go fast, go slow.

Drink it down, knock it back.
Sun comes up, afterglow.

Seasick

A slab of Dutch Gold and watch the night unfold.
Just kids on the lash, down around.
Revellers, swingers, shakers,
Pub to pub, chasing the music makers.
Blue sky over the Metalman.
We beat our chest and confessed;
Blessed by who we were and
Who we were gonna be.
At 17,
Skipping down the hill on Queen Street,
Crawling back up it hours later.
Tramore was the epitome of July and
We were set. We were gonna fly
Above the sand dunes. We were gonna be sky
High.
Skinning up, another sup. "Mup," I said,
"We'll sleep when we're dead."
Not a care by the sea air,
Watching the smoke from cigarettes
Dissipate into the night air.
In the beer garden of The Vic,
We trawled every pub for every sound, for every
melody, to waste our youth. Just hoors who were
cute and, we won't refute the drunken
confessions we released into the ether.
From The Shanty to the High Bee, breathe in, we're
Free. Night is young; just you wait and see.
High stools and pissed up fools, fake ID, keep it

tidy.

We did love to be beside the seaside, with eyes
wide, on those waves we were gonna glide, let
our worries slide, the moon in the sky our guide.
Run but never hide, our horizon was wide, time on
our side.

Watching it not get dark till after ten.

Youth was our trick. The dawn came in quick,
Like the tide on the beach when the night was
out of reach

And, when the sun came up, we were still young
But seasick.

Die Young

When the priest sprinkled the baptism water
upon your head,
As your parents held you proudly in a packed
church,
Was it already anointed that you would die young?
That you would go to the grave before your own
parents?
In the same church, you were baptised in a white
shawl, they would place your coffin beside the
same font that blessed your short time here.

We weren't made to die young:
To be disentangled from ceilings where we hung,

As a last gasp escaped your lung.
We weren't made to die young.
The broken generation
Where the tragic swallowed the magic of our
youth.
And all our dreams became worries and ghosts
that would haunt you in the dead of night.
And the sun was suffocated behind dark
clouds, and our bliss was choked by an empty
abyss that would claim the best and brightest.
They never said, you were gonna die young.
They never said, you'd be back here in a coffin
before you even got a chance to stand at an altar,
clutching the love of your life.

The novenas never said, you were gonna die young.
That you would appear on a Mass card before
you even got a 21st card.
They never tell us we die young.
They never say, the dawn won't rise before the
wolves claw away at your bones and they never
say, you'll just be another face in the death
notices, another statistic, another that lost their
way.
They never said, the team would have to carry you
draped in the club's colours or, that we'd watch
you return to the soil.
They never said, you cried yourself to sleep and
found it hard to leave your bed because, you were
broken. Now, we're all broken because, they never
said, you didn't want to stay.
They never said, we'd have to place your picture
on a coffin to a packed congregation.
They never said, we die young.

Late Night Letters

Have you ever been afraid
Of what they say and what they think,
Hiding behind drink,
Waiting for the insecurity to shrink?
Did you ever go looking for your tribe,
Feeling lonelier than words can describe?
Or, any poetry can surmise?
Staring at your ceiling,
Waiting for the sun to rise:
What's truth and what's lies?
And how you can never tell
What's behind anyone's eyes?
Did you ever feel lonely and
Lose the faith? Got in a state
Waiting for it to abate?
Crying for no reason:
The anxiety taunting and teasing
Because, to feel any other way was treason.
Did you ever find your way back,
After you've been the train
That veered off the track
And the bombs reigned down
And you were under attack, as the odds would
stack
But, you found your way back?
Did you ever jump headfirst
Into whatever made you afraid
Then, dust yourself off, wipe the sweat and the tears,

Pick yourself up off the ground?
This is how I'm made
And fear may recede, re-emerge, then fade.
Did you ever walk out into the world
Head high and whisper,
I'm not afraid?

All I Want for Christmas

All I want for Christmas
Is a roof over my head and a warm bed,
Money in my pocket, a winning docket.
All I want for Christmas
Is another month. The oncologist was blunt
When he told me, "You won't see Christmas."
For I won't wallow in woe;
I'll face bravely into the dark night but, I'm not
ready to go.
All I want for Christmas
Is to get off my face, another pill, another bag,
Another reason to give the demons in my head
Chase.
All I want for Christmas is to stop myself from
Crying. I'm telling all and sundry, I'm fine but really,
I'm lying – can't face Christmas; can't face the
tinsel and fairy lights, the long dark nights.
All I want for Christmas
Is to tuck my kids into warm beds
And not a bus shelter, to give them a home to lay
their head, to not roam the streets fearing the
evening's dread for, I'm a good mother and he's a
good father. What did we do to deserve this? All I
want for Christmas is a moment of bliss and, I'm
laying here in a cold sleeping bag, wishing on
stars at 3am, telling God, I've paid my due, when I
hear a taxi drive past and Shane McGowan
singing from the radio,

"I can see a better time, when all our dreams come true."

Twenty-One

We had the Dublin night in the palms of our hands
When we glared at the Liffey, over Capel Bridge
And raised hell on Parliament Street, like only we
could, like no one else would.
The night ahead of us, seduced by the lights and
the boys in drag. Oh, how my eyes would light up
like fireworks, swaying with a boy in The George
before he leaned in and kissed me and I still
tremble over the way he held my hand in an after-
midnight taxi back to Finglas and, how my heart
soared 'cos I've scored and adored the blue-
eyed boy who stole my heart on Capel Street,
and blessed his bedsheet.
When we were young, we thought we'd live
forever, love forever on heaving dancefloors,
dancing to bubblegum pop. The glory that was
bestowed upon me, on warm Dublin nights, were
the most beautiful sights, that cleansed my
weary eyes when the walls closed in and the
lights dimmed and, the cruel black taunted me
But, what a curtain call for, I wanted it all and, I'll
return soon and, by God I'll soar and raise a
drink to the nights we took the piss on the
Nitelink.
For the bars and streets of Dublin, the night owls
and the 6am faint sun over the Liffey were my
first love, parting ways with a one-night stand on
Patrick Street, another warm sheet. One never

Forgets for, I have no regrets for the drunken
chatter through 4am Stoneybatter. The moon like
a shield as we strutted through Smithfield for, I
have no regrets – I was only 21.

Agoraphobia

21.

When the sky fell in and I bolted the front door
And hid away from the world.
A fear of fear, here comes the tear.
What do you do when you get so scared?
These four walls keep the demons at bay.
Life was that thing on the other side of the front
door and yet, I was on the floor, in pieces
Falling apart in my bedroom.
Can't tell anyone: they'll all think I'm off me head.
Who the fuck doesn't leave their home?
Who the fuck can't walk around the corner before
the panic sets in? You're gonna lose control.
You're gonna end up on the pavement, catch your
breath, catch your death, shuffling, fidgeting. I'm
panicking. I'll never get home. I won't make it
home. I won't. I'm lost. I can't make the
appointment. "Dad, I'm sorry. I'm letting everyone
down. I can't make the 21st. I can't make my own
grandmother's funeral. I'm sorry, I'm letting
everyone down." I'm down. Breathe, just breathe.
I'm terrified. I'm terrified. I can't leave the house
because I'm terrified. I can't get in the car. I'm
terrified.
Pills and potions, torch songs and novenas.
Why me?
I lost my twenties – best years of your life, or so
they say. Come what may, I watched lives play

out on social media. I wished I was one of those lives. I wished I was at that concert, at that 21st, in that relationship, in that picture with some world famous landmark.

Me and the four walls, the no missed calls, my darkened halls but see, through it all, one thing I never lost was my balls.

'Cos it was Hell on Earth. It was isolation. My life was in desolation but, I had no choice but to tackle the white noise.

I am not living like this; I am not living.

21.

12 years.

The best prescription I ever got was my family. You can never get that the time back. There is only lost time that you can never make up and, then you wake up. I didn't dream it; I lived it.

It took 12 years, a million tears – too many, ten a penny. I crawled. I banged my head against brick walls, swallowed falls, internal brawls, no missed calls.

And here we are. I didn't dream it: my hometown glory, my story. I walked through and I'm not looking back. The blink of an eye, I start again.

I'm on the other side of the fear, back at the start, new items in the cart.

Agoraphobia, fear of open spaces yet, I've got an open heart, open mind, open mouth, open book.

Everything happens for a reason; I just know it happened.

Agoraphobia – beated it, completed it.

Fear is overrated. Love is underrated.

I didn't dream it.

About the Author

Wayne Power is a writer, poet and spoken word artist based in Waterford city.

Having studied journalism in Colaiste Dhulaigh in Dublin, he won a Sean Dunne Young Writers Award in 2002 for Best Local Prose. In 2019, through the Modwords collective, he burst onto the spoken word scene at a rapid pace. He quickly became a regular face at Waterford's various open mic nights, taking every opportunity to share his truths.

Within a few months, he had curated two Speakers Cormer spoken word and poetry events in collaboration with with Central Arts and their annual *Summer in the City* programme. Shortly after, he went on to MC their monthly open mic nights.

In April 2019, he launched the *Sound Up* podcast to highlight Waterford's thriving music and arts scene. The Sound Up Sessions were launched in March 2020 in Katty Barry's – a night of music and spoken word alongside local singer-songwriters, Mark Walsh and Ciaran Delaney.

He would write and star in his first short play, *Well Girl, Any News?*, which played as part of Modwords Festival in the Theatre Royal, Waterford in July 2019.

His poetry and writing are unfiltered, at times gritty, recalling lost nights, love, mental health and political themes coupled with a comedic edge, all of which celebrate the human condition. They are snapshots of the light and shade of city life, steeped in a fondness for where he is from, where he's been and where he hopes to go.

Wayne Power lives in Waterford and was proudly educated at Mount Sion, a school that produced one of the city's finest wordsmiths in the late Sean Dunne.

His debut collection, *Everyone's A Star After Midnight*, is dedicated to the underdogs, the dreamers, the mental health warriors, the unrequited, the shoulders we cry on and the torch songs we let heal us, the friends who become family and the family who become everything.

The cover shot and photography was produced by his beloved best friend, Hayley K Stuart.